WORD MUSIC

Hubert N. Newman

ORIGINAL WRITING

ISBN: 978-1-907179-80-8

A CIP catalogue for this book is available from the
National Library.

Published by Original Writing Ltd., Dublin, 2010.

Printed in Great Britain by MPG BOOKS GROUP,
Bodmin and Kings Lynn

To the memory of my parents
Nettie and Victor J. Newman, P.C

Acknowledgements

My thanks to Garrett Bonner and Steven Weekes for their assistance in the preparation and publication of this anthology.

CONTENTS

WORD MUSIC

A la recherche in Dublin...

Dublin isn't the same at all
As I pass by the long, long wall,
That capsule of Trinity Green.
But the view from Kildare hasn't changed
From Dáil to TCD.
Old Bewley's lost for evermore -
Shadow coffee of yore,
Your tobacco juice burned us,
Your buns shrank and turned us,
So out went the characters,
The craic and the chisellers,
The students, the poets,
The girls, and the boys.
Why should prosperity sour our honey,
Ireland once free, enslaved by money!
But Stephen's Green is as bonny as ever,
With kids breading ducks
Where the green is so green,
And the calm is so peaceful
Against the cauldron-bubble
Of the new Dubh-linn,
Jostling and crowded,
A people enshrouded.
From Tallaght to Connolly,
Sandyford to Stephen,
The stuffed lives trundle,
Packed with body and bundle,

No matter the time
That the calling bells chime.
I would have thought it a dream,
A sky postcard-blue
In a Dublin summer
By my childhood duck-water
In that heart-centre Square.
Now we've all played here,
Three generations of innocent joy
From the stout soul of Corkonian boy.

A THOUGHT

How frail our soul
  Its fragile links
    A prey to solitude.

Love is its breath
  A wife, a child,
    A prayer to its God.

A silken web
  Of falsity
    Is all a man can build,

To gird himself
  With paltriness.
    Trade warmth of heart for gold.

A network of
  Complexity
    Becomes a living shroud,

Entombs the human
  Vanity
    And snaps the pulsing thread.

Spring awakening

How sensed the beauty of the petalled spring,
   Its graceful fragrance glistening through the rain
      To penetrate the sunless sky!

Those speckled blinding bands that warm the eye,
   Those blossom clouds suspended from the trees,
      Then carpetting the plain dull earth -

They weave a fantasy of light and life,
   A mellow harmony in mind and eye,
      A melody for nature and for me.

Autumn Leaves

Spring's breath lies hot on autumn's brow
  Whispering remember,
Reluctant yields her budding warmth
  To the embrace of September,

Whose blissful calmness casts its spell
  Through ripening shades of gold
And russet spread on forest fields
  Her promise unfulfilled,

Till the rich speckled jewekkery,
  Green by nature's alchemy transmuted,
Descending on the wind's soft sigh,
  A gilded veil for earthen sorcery.

RAILWAY REFLECTION

Dusk descending over still grey ribbons
Winding through the living land,
Its meshwork sparkling like fireflies,
The wanderings of mankind.
I woonder whether in that vast assembly
There is one who knows his station,
Or are all overwhelmed by their own knowledge,
Those self-appointed masters of Creation.

To me the quiet of the autumn sky
Is master of my mind.
These things mine, the rest I leave
To waste their hour in metaphysic strife.

HOMAGE

Who can match the spot kaleidoscope
Of an impressionist!
A vivid sea of multicoloured drops
That near the eye perplex, but viewed from far.
Assume a form revivifying life,
And soulful, with the artist's heart imbued -
A precious thing portrayed with camel hair,
Or by the genius of a dying body,
With fever, covering walls, doors, backs of chairs,
With sticks and human hair for brushes,
And with lifeblood for paint.

TIME

Those precious hours that waste away
With fatal indecision,
And timorous doubts that strain our souls
Entrapped, yet full of giving.

WINTER

What a time of year to set to poetry -
A harsh, ill-tempered season, prima donna,
Fitful and moody, given to depression,
Unaccountable, and sword sharp blizzard storms
Untempered, uncontrollable. How false
The flitting silence of the snow.

Your breath
Scarce taken than the savage scudding clouds
Wreak wintry havoc on the nests and burrows
Where huddle humanity, and many other species,
Some even nobler, though say it in a whisper,
Lest you prick his conceit.

Maybe it's time
Most meet to think, and set it down in words,
When the keen-bladed, icy-whetted air
Edges the mind so that it sees more piercing
Through the frail self-deceptions of our lives.

The sundered day of rest, and all lies hushed
In the noontime sun of dawning spring,
While the mingling vapours of the seasons
Blanket the town below, so that its lines
Are blurred, as our horizons by our frailty.

Snow

It is not like the other elements,
But brings a change upon the yielding earth,
Covering its bareness with a feathered tapestry
Of glacial purity, misleading beauty,
But proof, unyielding to soft living warmth.

The harsh cold wind of winter dies away,
And in its place strange sprites slip silently,
And mischievous tangle with the dancing flakes,
Scattering the jewelled gossamer

From the grey fleece of winter-clouded heaven,
Flluttering merrily through the hushed, still air,
Until its mystic spell enshrouds the land
So silently, and to our wondering eye
Unfolds a frigid beauty.

Shall we then
Find pleasure in the graceful forest limbs,
Their browns clothed delicate in virgin white;
The lacy quilted fields, the orange glow
Of pale sun orb in ashen evening sky?

Or has the marble cold another embrace
That stills the life force with a mortal chill?

West Country Summer

The orange blossom of a summer sky
Lies pure serene upon a human haze,
Which shades the quiet view that meets our gaze
Over the hills of our west-country home.

Each village swelters in the humid valley,
Unless blessed by Mendip breeze along the moors.
Follow the Avon on its tortuous route
Through narrow channel and 'tween towering cliffs

To sandy shores of Severn water flowimg
From the heights of Wales. They make a sight
Those cliffs bedecked by nature and by man
With trees and caves. And from the bridge seen all

A spreading city, once the bustling home
Of England's pride, and still in the rough country
Betwen Cotswolds and Mendips, stretching its growing fringe
As far as the eye can see from Cabot's tower.

There's a garden! Flowered waterfalls
And soothing shades, the freshness of flowing water,
And children playing. The gentle air of peace
In such a summer captures the joy of living.

Rendezvous

We are here, we go there,
Have no fear, for we share
Strange times together
In fair and foul weather.
That voice says: take care,
Let you both be aware,
So you live long-life measure
For work, and for pleasure.
From sadness came love,
Deceit from above,
And all one's alarms
Falsely soothed by fake charms
Of voice, mind and soul,
Should have made our minds whole.
And I stand astride
Lone, the onrushing tide.

Quizzical

How could one not love
   This one, so warm, inviting,
Sent from up above,
   And it can read your writing.

To walk, talk, rest together,
   In peace-happy pleasure,
To traverse April weather
   And savour July treasure.

To rise early morning
   From cosy at night,
Work and play dawning,
   Be it sun, moonlit night.

The Captain

Like a ship with no rudder
Are sister and brother,
No Captain on bridge anymore.

The navigator's left,
And it's we are bereft,
Though he's rested on safe-harboured shore.

The sea's all around us,
Shoals and shallows to ground us,
And we've lost our Pilot of life,

Who threaded our green minds
Through life's channel-strewn mines,
Ever shielding his loved ones from strife.

The grandchildren he knew
May be four and two,
But their Papa's a memory they share,

Kind, alive, always smiling,
Those blue eyes still beguiling,
Blue child eyes, young and old, pure and rare.

And, though the Captain's at rest,
We, his offspring, do our best
To navigate his chart as he'd wanted.

Though his life-chart be worn,
May his children be borne
Safely on, that his wishes be granted!

Aegaean Harmony

The table-shaded mountain glimmers
As we glide past on blue foamed sea;
Grey-brown hills in sunlit shimmers,
Aegaean peace, not love, but free!

Those sun-stroked slopes with speckled green
Hillside farms and nestling homes,
Island of cats and donkeys, seen,
Safe, secure, beneath whitened domes.

Troubled nation, now at rest,
Invasions, insurrections over,
Be at peace, I hope, not least,
For you yourselves, and this sea rover.

A Lesson from the Black Watch

All I desire is to be left in peace:
Thus spoke my Father and old Wellington.
These the words of heroes, sung, unsung,
Risked their all for what they knew was right.
Didn't give a damn about the mob,
Cynical, saw the decadence that would follow
When lowest common denominator ruled the land,
And knew to treat the idiocy of inferiors
With amused tolerance, as they pruned their roses.

A Son's Pain

It is terrible, to me such a man should die,
To pass, simultaneous, to Sovereign Lord and earth:
I pray his goodness and his wisdom counted
In worth Above, though lost to me below.

Left low in a quandary of loneliness,
Encroached on by billions, yet a solitary soul,
Unwilling left, who cannot plumb his memories,
Who taught me all I know that is worthwhile.

In silver salts and oils his smile surrounds me,
His voice still guides me on life's chartless path.
However fleeting he touched the rare good soul,
Yet pierced his blue eyes their everlasting memory.

He was not heard by those who should have listened,
The inevitable fate of all true prophets,
Like them, proclaimed the path of forthright principle
To stiff-necked, never those to reckon truth.

Yet his is that echoing voice of the millennia,
Unobscurantist, ringing strong and true:
I, one of the few who listened,
Bitter regret I did not listen more.

Listening

That were peace enough
Soft stirring of the fire against the gentle melody,
And all the world outside.
Our harmony unfettered,
Love's listening notes exploring every echo
Of living restlessness.
That part of us
That never comes to life once we have left
Our childhood innocence,
Unless Heaven bless
Our brief and fleeting hour with pleasant chords.

February

I watch the sleek, soft down upon the lake
   That glides on the glassy cold,
Ruffled by the north whose shiver-bitter breath
   Ensheaths the new spring fold

Struggling to raise the warmth of life reborn,
   Impatient of winter's chains,
How brave the saffron heralds of the spring
   Call for April's gentle rains.

I know that all the budded greenery
   Has learned its lesson well,
Will not be lured by icy treachery
   To unfold its verdant shell

To a sky whose blue is scarred by steely grey,
   Whose gold is chill, whose reds betoken snow:
They wait expectant till its iron-clad veil
   Be cast to darkness by the rosy brow

Of spring.

STILL WINTER

I hear the song that falls among the flowings
   Of the chill forest streams,
The plaintive curlew, and the bold bright colours
   Of the pale heaven gleams.

I hear the call of earth for it is close to man,
   Even when the tinsel grey
Blends with a feeble sun on a smoke horizon
   On a pastoral winter's day.

Meaning

The whole of existence is made of days,
Each with its measure of sadness and joy,
So much labour, so much rest and thought.
You bid farewell to home to earn your livelihood,
To keep yourself and those you love from want,
Mind and body free from earthly care.
Vain aspiration or the only vision
Worthy of him who calls himself a man?
One could view the daily cycle of events
As endless. spiralling perpetual motion,
A road without escape and without pleasure,
As if you were only born to stumble headlong
Onwards into manhood and the grave,
Or you could value every moment like a jewel,
Your life being the most precious gem you have.

Seasonal

Welcome to high noontime,
  My summer friends,
So short in this clime,
  For such happiness ends

Quickly, leaving the soul
  Dancing in anguish,
Heeding the summer call,
  Leaving to languish

The temperate lands of the north,
  Where pleasures are few, but sweet calm
Reigns supreme, while the swift ventures forth
  To warmth, ocean blue, but the palm

Of the tropics, torrid and fevered,
  Both nature and man of a kind,
Places where peace never weathered
  The frays of monsoon or mankind.

THE MUSE

Poetry flows only from troubled souls,
Verses from sorrow, joy or outraged hearts,
But not when inner self is most disturbed,
Numbed by excess of love or tragedy.
For when the tempest rages in your soul,
Words ill portray your mind, far less false rhyming.
Yet this strange medium of coupled sounds
Is an outlet for those lesser times of day
When, though a vast emotion shakes the frame,
Lighter burdens find their best expression
In even the simple rhythm of my verse.

OH NO, THE BUILDERS...

On ladder to ceiling
To hang up that net,
When you should be feeling
The warmth of a jet

Of water refreshing
And bubble bath foam,
As you wait for the crashing
Of tiles in your home.

But, don't worry a damn,
It's not as bad as it seems,
Fill the gaps with amalgam
And you'll have sweet dreams.

Life and Love and Love of Life

Sunshine, cold, or stormy weather,
Sleet, or rain, or hail, or snow,
What matters is - you are together,
For living life is here and now.

With the queues and shopping over
There is time to slow your walk -
Time spent best in love's endeavour -
Well met eyes, and silent talk.

Through the fray, from pain to calm,
Days hard-won from tears and toil,
Happy days, without alarm,
Fruits won from a cloying soil.

You've had your share of wear and tear -
At least you've lived to love as far.

Teenage Verdure

This ancient oak ascending by my eyes,
Old symbol of the beauty of this land,
Whose firm broad trunk and slender branches rise
Revealing to me the Greatness of That Hand
Has stood in stately majesty and gazed
For centuries on those who walked beneath,
By all this pulsing greenwood life amazed
As by the woodland scents that caught their breath.

How fleeting and ephemeral are we
When cast against the stoutness of the trees!
Has not our race some strong desire to be
As pure, unspoiled of substance, as are these?
Alas the sorrowing waste of all our powers
Given in Unseen bounty to our race
Senselessly spurned even our waking hours
Seeking to scatter the forest's life-giving trace.

Present Future

Cyberspace is not the way
   To help our love stay strong,
Nor work the cure to pass the day
   When absence makes us long,

For we have been through earthly fires
   And suffered heart and mind
Through pains that cut and grief that tires,
   And yet no-one will find

As pure and true united two
   Who through the fray have come,
And now, please God, a happier day
   Dawns with their joining home.

No longer children but full grown,
   I think we understand
Inseparable, not on our own
   Entwined, and hand in hand.

Before Temple Bar

City of light and a hundred rainbows.
Gleaming and twinkling like the azure above,
Dazzling my eyes through the stained glass windows
Of the old established 'Turtle and Dove.'

City of sound and a thousand laughters
Echoing eerily from Liffey bounds
Coming back to shake the gnarled oak rafters
Resounding to the cries of 'last one round!'

City of touch and a million paws
Clasped round the handle of the pewter mug
Soon to be voided down capacious jaws
Familiar to the eyes of the Toby Jug.

How low, you think, my inspiration's sunk
Perhaps, for once, I am a - little - drunk!

CATS

There was a friendly pussy
  That sat upon a wall.
It really was quite fussy
  Which side of it to fall.

Its whiskers twitched with worry,
  Which human might feed best.
It's coat was bristling furry,
  It couldn't get much rest.

Bot now its problem's over,
  The neighbour's come to stay,
So it can jump right over,
  Eat, and then to play.

It only goes to show, dear,
  That nine lives for a cat
Mean far more than a miaou, dear,
  All curled up on a mat.

A Sonnet

The heart no master knows but its desire
  No sooner seen than wanted,
And perishes consumed by its own fire
  Unless that wish is granted.

And so it is when innocent and free
  Your honest path is crossed
And purpose, life itself and liberty
  Are thrown as gages to be won or lost.

Depending on the clouded hand of fate
  For all his future hopes,
Forsaking reason and with faltering gait
  The lover like a blind man gropes,

Uncertain of reward yet confident,
Imperious love can not face banishment

Moods

Unaccountable the times that deep depression
Steals into mortal mind. I know no hour
But that I wish to add to my contentment,
To give my soul peace. But what, indeed, is peace
Or joy? Though humble, yet I feel I sense
The meaning of our lives, at least that part
That best deserves our thoughts. So I'll not pass
Vain hours in speculation,metaphysics
But rather move in moods of harmony
With other souls brought close to mine by weathering.

LE SINGE ET LES SOURIS

Or, il y avait deux souris
   Qui bagarraient violemment
Au sujet d'un joli fromage.
   S'étant battues toute la nuit,
Elles sont allées au tribunal
   Pour décider
A qui était ce beau Cantal.
Le juge qui était singe
   A bien failli se briser les méninges
     En décidant
       A ce sujet.
Enfin il était prêt
   Et, prenant le fromage,
Il l'a coupé en deux,
   En a pesé les deux morceaux.
Cette action aurait été sage,
   Mais, dommage,
Les morceaux étaient toujours inégaux.
   N'importe, a dit monsieur,
Et, en soulevant le plus grand,
   Il en a pris
     Un petit peu
Et l'a mangé.
   Malheureusement,
Les moceaux étaient toujours inégaux!

Pourtant il a continué
    A grignoter dans ce fromage:
Il n'en restait la moindre partie.
Alors, mesdames, le juge a dit,
J'espère après ce petit tour
Que vous n'irez plus à la cour.

Snow

So silent hushed descending from a steel-grey sky,
   Soft swirling vaporous mist of fragile flakes.
Breathless lies nature rapturous expectantly,
   Embellished snow beauties on the unruffled lake.

Where each fairy falling drop of diamond pure
   Glides noiselessly into the motionless deep,
Phantom mystic shroud of winter-false allure
   Lulling ife into light lethe unsuspecting sleep.

White flowing tears adorn the winter willows
   Submissive bowing their slender arching limbs
Towards the budding fields with fresh spring furrows
   While the scent of ramrod pines still upwards climbs

With their gently swaying hands of green and white.
   The earth cracks crisp and clean beneath your feet,
And strong clear cold meets rosy cheeks, and sparkling sights
   Glisten on trees shorn of their leafy coats.

DESIRE

An empty house
  A lonely mind,
A loving soul
  That yearns to find
Another heart
  Of crystal pure,
Of gentle grace
  And sweet allure.
So dreamt I on a foreign strand,
So dream I now in my own land.

Music hath charms...

Vivaldi's chords and Bach's melodious trills
Fall on my ear like dancing autumn leaves,
Like shimmering droplets from the mountain sills
Where first I found that music that bereaves

The mind of care, the tired flesh of toil,
That stirs rejoicing in the human heart.
Gladness, thanksgiving pur out from the soil
We are, out by the only art

The only vent our human selves can find
To truly express the emotions that we feel,
The bursting love, the overflowing joy,
And everlasting praise to God on high!

A SONNET

It were no wonder in our present age
To mock and scorn, as countless, mindless fools,
At ancient custom, knowledge and adage,
Of life-buildig the power and the tools.

To plunder, uproot, ravage and destroy,
Staggering bloodsoaked guilty through the spoil
Of countless centuries of laborious joy
And worldwide monuments to patient toil.

The all-knowing present spurns the humble past,
The upstart struts where nobles feared to tread,
The two-faced hypocrite stands, supreme at last,
And solitary virtue hides in dread.

Yet even now a handful stem the flood
Of evil, by the eternal force of good.

FATHER

Dear Dad, your wisdom comes into my mind
   When I attune my ear to hear your voice,
Gentle, thoughtful, prudent, firm, and kind,
   Wise in advice, but always leaving choice.

And, when you had to go, you left me one
   And, through her, two so special to my heart.
While I can stand, let no man stand alone,
   But from his dearest never be apart.

Block or chip, that sister mine is yours
   In all the character she got from you,
And so comes it two blessed girls are hers,
   Keeping those traditions you kept, true.

And when, as every day, we turn our souls
   For guidance to the one whom we have lost,
We feel his spirit enter to our souls
   As always, bringing help when needed most!

IF

If were a word to tangle with,
In despair for hope,
In joy for sadness,
Ever giving birth to dreams of gladness.
I am so, but, if I were such and such,
If I had scope, if I had much
I would do more than I have ever done.
If only this were otherwise.
Thus turning self-deceiving lies
Into a feeble mask for human frailty.
If is the excuse for inability
To think, to ask, to do or say
To pass in happiness the livelong day
If I were here,
If I were there,
If I were where
I am not now.
And so
We pass our days
Philandering with life,
And in our sightless ways
We engage in strife.
Cursed ambition and discontent
When beyond all bounds they stray.
Let moderation rule your course
Through life, and bear in mind the Source
Whence comes reward and true content.

Joy is a blessing from above
Accompanying health, and peace, and love.
Don't pass your life in idleness
Of ifs, for there is naught
That man can gain by wishful thought.

Festive Season

Were it not the sadness of my loss
And absence of the one who is not near,
I could be happy at this time of year,
After all, it is a festive season -

A festival of lights in wax and heart,
When shortening days have gone, and wintry sun
Sends longer beams into our weathered souls,
Cracking the ice of January chill.

The glittering hoar frost crunching beneath our boots
Cannot quench the flames of pending spring,
The plans of upland pleasure that will come,
For life's to live and love and be contented,

So many pleasures to fulfill our beings.
So let it happen, winter, spring and all,
From homely chores to dinners for our friends,
From quiet twosome to the crowded scene,

Most time for the romance of the soul,
Equal at work or in our private room,
Fulfillment of the mind and of the flesh.
Day or night at home, or other parts.

Above all we're amused and share a laugh,
A sip of bubbly and a bite together,
Cheerful words, a shedding of day cares,
And, afterwards, a silent blissful warnth.

WINTER

Clouds and darkness on the land,
All of a sudden winter's here.
The panoply of autumn bland
Lies rotting in the forests sere.
Chill blows the wind,
A snowy blanket hides the ground
And muffles every sound
Of forest prowler, wolf and fox,
Winding stealthily round tthe rocks
In search of spoil.
Shorn of their summer splendour
The trees stand gaunt against an ashen sky.
The blizzard hurls itself in fury blind
Against their poor bare wooden armoury.
Now see nature pour
Her violence on life.
Now witness the eternal strife,
The struggle for existence.
Like some great ship astride an angry sea,
Trusting for safety only in Providence,
Tossing and twisting as the billows roar,
And round its sides the waters boil
Encasing it in furious foam,
So trust Nature's children
Huddling for comfort in snowy burrows
Beneath leafless boughs bending in the wind.
Shall they again

Forget their sorrows
In the hope of Spring?
No-one can find
In all this sombre cloudiness
The faintest glimmer of a silver lining.
Even the humble snowdrop hides its head.
Our summer visitors have flown in dread
Of winter's numbing touch.
Only cock sparrow and robin chirp defiance,
And animals of prey now make alliance,
Desperate for survival.
Now the snowflakes cease to fall
And all the air again is still
Save for the mountain waterfall
And the rushing, icy sill.
The lake is coated with a glassy sheet,
The land with a blanket virgin-white,
A phantom stillness holds the scene in thrall,
The country lies imprisoned in this gaol
Of silence,
And all that shrouded living might
Lies hidden like an army inderground,
Awaiting from their Leader one small sound
To burst those manacles of chilly cold,
Don life and strength new-found,
And shine forth splendid in veronal gold.

SPRING

Spring is the glorious time
Of promise full and fair,
When in our temperate clime
April sprinklings fill the air
With the sweet odour of renewing life,
And the brief sunshine, always too sparse
Bestows its long-sought beams
On meadow and garden grass.
We fill our heads with dreams.
Strong tender buds burst from the earth.
The air is filled with sound,
All nature's progeny embroiled in strife
Amiable that there should be no dearth
Of beauty rising from the fertile ground.
Over hills and meadows,
Mountains and streams,
Rush torrents and rivulets,
Fresh from their sources,
Coursing and rolling along by the hedgerows,
The crystal-clear mountain sill spangles and gleams,
Entwining the greenery with silver necklets,
Down, down from the mountainside hurriedly courses.
This lifeblood of nature
Will mingle with the sun rays rare,
And nurse alike with care
Tall trees and field-wild- fare.

Now in the soft spring pasture
Life abounds.
The farmer renews his task.
On blossomed ground
The lovers walk.
The questions that they ask
Each other in their earnest talk
Will find the purest answers that they may
In the contentment of a summer's day.

SUMMER

There is a rarity in our brave land,
It is the summer season.
But those of us whose lives have spanned
More than a decade can recall
On the far distant horizon
The blissful calmness of a summer's day
With all the world at peace.
Young and old, all life at play
As if happiness should never cease.
All through the woodland tall
Crowned with refreshing emerald hue,
A golden haze descends upon the fields
Embalming all in living folds.
Like a protective covering it shields
The earth from cold.
Only a gentle breeze disturbs the calm,
Ruffling noiselessly through the growing green.
Pan sends upon the air a melody
Which, with its lyric haunting harmony,
Enchants all living, casting mystic spells
Of bliss and incantation magical,
Weaves joyful robes for nature's family,
Wreathing all necks with flowers, with smiles all faces,
Fills every heart with gladness overflowing,
And every eye uplifted heavenward
Pours forth its praises in a thankful torrent
To the Creator of this glimpse of paradise.

But in this our northern land,
Rare like an orchid amazonian,
The sun never sends its wanted golden beams
Until after hours of weary loitering
We reach our home late, and look upon those beams
Of fickle contrariety that fan
Our waning hopes like dying embers. Sudden,
Shimmering sunlight fills a roseate sky
With promise all but certain that the morn
Like some exotic flower will open wide
In all its glory, and the graceful dawn
Like some pert maid of oriental pride
Will rise from sleep in jewelled ecstasy,
Golden Aurora with resplendent radiance
Reflected in the diamond dew of earth.
The morrow then we rise and all the promise
Was not false, for there before our eyes
Unfolds a panoply of beauty unimagined
That does all senses with its splendour satiate.
For now the sun in summer's robes arrayed
Rises majestic over the eastern sky,
Sends forth its warmest and most kindly beams
To nourish the land, and with seasoned content
Gladden our hearts and put our minds at peace.
Like some fine tapestry of eastern weave.
Enriched with colour as a bird of paradise,
A layer of flowered glory hides the ground.

Late magnolia delicate pastel blooms
Open their beauty to the morning air.
Roses' richly petalled fragrance
Adorns with perfumed air the atmpsphere.
Unwonted songsters add their notes of joy
To the unrivalled chorus of the sky.
The beauty of this time shall be
New strength to youth nd comfort to old age.
You and I, meandering in its midst,
Shall feel the furrows smoothed from off our brow.
The summer breeze, like musical melodious,
May charm away some trouble from our lives,
And with the sweet soothing hand of kind oblivion
Banish unhappiness, and with gentle love
Bestow contentment on the young at heart.

Autumn

The blithe forgetfulness of summer days
Blends with the calm tranquillity of fall.
The sun, scarce less luxurious in its warmth,
Still shines in spendour on a radiant earth.
But now the more gaudy panoply of youth
Has faded, and mature serenity
Enfolds all nature in her fond embrace.
The wild exuberance of veronal days
Lies ripening in the fresh fertile ground.
Harvest fields lie carpeted beneath
A shower of rustling russet gold that hid
The branches of the forest from all gaze
Unkind, and now the fruitful golden fields
In their turn hides. The love that bloomed in spring
Now walks enchanted in the orchard air
Beneath boughs burdened with firm freshness,
Succulent fruits that scent the cloistered walks
Where Eros laughing plays with merry bow.
All nature conspires to make the earth
Yield forth due sustenance, so that all life
Shall not lie helpess in cold winter's grasp.
Mellowed by a season's age, the land has shed
Its coat of many colours. Brighter hues
Of former days lie treasured in the memory,
And, like the jewelled cover of a book
Of antique rarity and precious soul,
The glories of the past lie gently folded

In an envelope of gently floating leaves
That lightly waft on an autumnal breeze,
Their russet tints outmatching any art,
A blend far finer than the hand of man
Could ever fashion. And shall we not stroll
In soft contentment through the calm still woods,
The crackle of fern and bracken beneath our feet,
The gracefully descending foliage,
Showering confetti-like its seasoned blessings
On all who search beneath for happiness
In this vast temple fashioned by the hand
Of nature? Lofty oak and humble moss
Sweet-scented pines affording thought to man,
And shelter to the creatures of the woods
Timidly rustling through the undergrowth
In search of succour against a harsher time.
Many a garden of town or country home
Now like a haven opens trellised gate
Festooned with roses or dark ivy eaves
To those in search of autumn quietude.
Such bowers are special to the heart of man,
They have about them some unearthly aura,
Some semblance to the paradise of Eden,
Where our first parents lived in unspoiled harmony.
Soft falls the pace on the green turf beneath,
Cascading mingling scent of fruit and flower,
The sound of droning bees, and singing birds

Which have not faithless flown to sunnier climes.
This wondrous tapestry by nature woven
Entwines the wanderer in its magic meshes,
And casts a spell of peace upon his soul.
This is the reaper's season, so shall he
Find rest for mind and body, and reward
For toil, and with his heavenly Maker
Renew the solemn covenant of life.

A Farewell

Though absent hearts be far away
  Yet we shall mot forget,
The happy moments of the day
  Shall not pass without regret.

And whether in Erin's Isle we meet
  Or in some alien land,
There'll be no want of smile to greet
  Old friendship's proffered hand.

May sweet contentment ve your lot
  Till our paths cross once more,
And since that is our dearest thought
  We'll wish you, not adieu, but au revoir.

Summer thoughts

Is life kind or nature cold?
  Even on a summer's eve
I can see a tale oft told
  Making me both joy and grieve.

For the night is still and calm
  In this sanctuary of peace.
Let no-one make alarm
  Lest the wonder should cease.

The water of the lake, like glass
  Reflects the bowing trees,
Dew blossoms on the grass,
  The blades stand straight, thee is no breeze.

Where once wildness reigned supreme,
  The hand of man has brought
Beauty from a dream
  And gardens from a thought.

Colour to outrun the eye,
  Perfume to fill the night,
And yet there is a sigh,
  And yet all is not right.

A hand gnarled by toil and age
   Fumbles for some bread,
A truce to the war we wage,
   Man and bird instead

Reach out. A glimpse of unity
   In the struggle for life,
A moment in eternity,
   A respite to strife.

THE CROSSROADS

It was the twilight hour, the traveller paused
Pensive in thought, as by the road ahead
Stood some strange signpost whose directions
Stayed never steadfast, but with varying hue
And quick succession cast their magic words
Before the traveller's eyes, now bright, now dark,
Now letters large as life itself, now small,
Retreating into the approaching night.
And on those signs no name of distant town,
But names and hopes that struck the very chord
Of harmony within the traveller's breast,
Name of his work, his present and his past,
Name of his love and of his future hopes.
The mocking shades grew ever larger now,
And with their fingers caught the glittering signs
And held them fast in the obscurity.
Despair in his heart the traveller turned his eyes
Pleading in prayer to Heaven, and lo, afar
On the horizon, like the glow of dawn,
With colour constant, not with flickering light,
Stood two forms wreathed in calm serenity.
One was called Peace, the other Happiness,
And all at once the signpost stood transfixed
And pointed clearly to the splendid vision,
And with strength in his limbs and purpose in his walk,
And with deep thankfulness, he set his course
Towards the forms, and the approaching dawn.

Evening in Dublin Bay

A mystery lies in the sea,
The source of all life,
Destroyer of proud and of free,
Young and old, man and wife.

Here its vastness unfolds 'neath a sky
Of a golden and summery hue.
What secrets are veiled to the eye
By that shroud of dull blue.

Onwards and ever onwards
Ploughing through foam and white spray,
Forwards and ever forwards
Goes the mariner's way.

Untold are the stories and treasures
That lie under the waves.
How deaf an ear turned to man's pleasures
By the dark ocean caves.

Now through the twilight's grey
Breaks a glimmer of gold,
Bringing fragments of warmth to the bay
So still and so cold.

The harbour lights twinkle and shine
And beckon you near.
Each beam lays a silvery line
To make the way clear

To the ships that will take you away
To a sunnier clime,
Lured by the spell of the sea,
As ageless as time.

A THOUGHT

Each man's the master of his destiny,
Each woman, too, the mistress of her own.
Let no-one fall ingloriously,
But, rather, stand alone.

THE VILLAGE INN
(WITH APOLOGIES TO GOLDSMITH AND GRAY)

Here in a tiny valley by the Seine
The district bistro held its drunken sway.
Long had its folding doors kept out the rain,
And welcomed travellers from the public way.

Today its portals know no sudden sound,
Its hinges rust from want of 'three in one,'
A pile of sodden fag ends hides the ground
That boots oflovesick Frenchmen trod upon.

Fled are the days when on the tables round
Stood glasses of bière and dil. vin rose,
Soon to be raised by hands tobacco-browned,
Then to find rest on tables cellulose.

Fled are the hours when after ten at night
Sat crowds of Paris workmen playing cards,
Poker and baccarat, each caused its separate fight,
All worthy subjects for Pindaric bards.

There in a corner sat the brawny Pierre,
Hero of a thousand bistro brawls,
His body, objet digne du dieu de guerre,
Has left its massive mark on these old walls.

Those other giants, Titas one and all,
Have wielded mighty arms about the room,
Wreaked havoc on the weaker that did call
To quench their thirst, only to meet their doom.

What epic deeds lie hidden 'neath the floor,
What souvenirs of French heroic fame
Lie buried, with a pile of louis d'or,
In fitting tribute to the patron's name!

What hearts of oak hae spewed the blood around
Those massive arteries encased in steel,
To muscles that did in mighty strength abound,
And of others of weaker oak the fate did seal.

 Now all those days of martial splendour past,
And all those hours of living legend o'er,
Let us evoke, we humble mortals last
Of all, the myth that sadly is no more.

Here in a tiny pool of water dark,
Steepéd in mud of origin obscure,
Primeval man decided to embark
On city building of construction pure.

Out of this teming filth and odorous dirt,
Aeolian splendours circling round her crown,
Arose a city with great towers girt,
Of Gallic tales the pride and the renown.

Like ancient Babel did its columns rise
In times when stalked proud Vercingetorix,
Ascending heavenward through the azure skies,
Inspired by architects, and occasonal bricks.

Paved were its streets in cobbled harmony,
Adornéd its walls with adverts manifold,
Ruléd its dwellings by la conciergerie
With honest hearts, and for substantial gold.

To one great man from out this noble flock,
Bacchus his name, his ptron Beelzebub,
Who revelled day and night on ancient hock,
There fell the honour, to erect a pub.

With Herculean siews, Titan might,
With solitary toil, blood, sweat ad tear.
He laboured to assuage the sorry plight
Of thirsty citizens with no place to beer.

Stone after stone, plank after plank impaled
With Stygian inexorableness unmatched,
It upwards mounted, to the sky unveiled,
Until the builder clothed the deficit with thatch.

Then came that day of splendour and renown
When all his mighty labours at an end,
Did lordly Bacchus don his kingly crown
And take up empire, and begin bartend.

Fast flowing, full and free, came crimson wine,
Sweet alcohol, both strong, weak, dark and pale.
Ere morning's chariot came with Queen Diane,
Found all but the hero in the city jail.

Here thou, great Bacchus, whom all men adore,
Hast wielded sceptre with unrivalled fame,
Adjudged libations with impartial score,
Maintained true stupor with unquenchéd flame.

Now read the incription on those ruins base,
With hanging plaster and with crumbling wall:
'No mortal man shall ever his name erase,
The noblest licensed vintner of them all.'

On Viewing the Harbour from the Summit of Howth Hill at Night

Not the quaint evening spell of the moon
On the harbour tonight,
But a magical mist from the gloom
Makes a silvery light

Which glows on the scene set below,
All a township asleep,
And the brave fishermen come and go
On the treacherous deep.

To the left and the right of the bar,
Like stars shine the warming beams,
Welcoming travellers from far
To a rest without dreams.

And the air now so calm and so still
And coloured with velvety grey,
Holding the landscape in thrall
Till the joy and the brightness of day.

Let the pulse of your heart join the waves,
And offer your soul to the night,
Free from a life that enslaves
And is blind to the wonders of sight!

A Sonnet

Will no-ne come and join me on the height
Of human life, to feel and share with me
Untold exquisite pleasure and delight,
Music to charm the soul to harmony.

So much of beauty to enchant the eye
And hold it in a speckled paradise,
Such pure, soft, sweet, soul-stirring melody
To call forth gladness from the worldly wise.

What wretched clay is he who is not turned
To wondrous forms by the gentle hand of art.
Pity the dull untutored mind that spurned
The hand of knowledge, for it is a part

Of life known to a few. The rest will die
In ignorance and blind obscurity.

Hope

Weary explorer in a trackless land,
The wandering soul alone its way must find,
Endlessly searching, groping, faltering hand
An eye unseeing along a path unsigned.

Unsounded depths and heights vertiginous
Peril the traveller's way at every pace,
Frail fragile heart to fall inglorious,
Exhausted, nor leave one despairing trace

Of struggles noble, though how impotent
Against remorseless Time's suspended sword,
Yet who so pressed but cannot find content
In life's horizons with a pleasant word,

A thought, a deed, to make a spark of warmth,
And stir life's ashes with renewing strength.

On the Coast of Brittany

Alone on the shore with a Celtic moon
And the roar of the oncoming tide,
Caught by the notes of a vibrant tune
As the soul of a man by his bride.

I look on the town now so calm and so still,
Held in the spell of the night,
Wreathed in soft purple and gold until
Dispelled by the dawning of light.

None break the peace but the sound of the sea
And the wind whipping chill through the air.
The children are sleeping who played merrily,
The beach lies deserted and bare.

Far out in the channel the ships come and go
To bring holidaymakers to France,
Setting their courses for old St. Malo,
Pirate town at the mouth of the Rance.

Veiled in grey mist the dark forms of the isles
Rise gloomy and cold in the bay,
The same as by day wreathed in sun-golden smiles
Set their charms to lure children to play.

And so the ephemeral grasp of our race
Is broken at this lonely hour,
Man's futile endeavours leave scarcely a trace
As Nature regains her mystrious power.

REFLECTION

Art, music, light, colour,
Sound, dazzling, glorifying,
Brilliant, blending, beautifying,
Joy, youth, heart, vigour,
Blinding flash inspiring,
Piercing laser-like the sapping gloom
Of a sickened world.

AWARENESS

Not a sound in all the night
But falls pleasant on my ear,
Not evil heard or in my sight
But is powerless to come near.

Strange the power that music has
To flow into the soul,
To cast oblivion on sad days,
To take possession and enthrall

In strains of harmony so pure
That bring man nearest to the Name,
A gentle insubstantial cure
For immaterial pain.

MORE PHILOSOPHY?!

Affection dies slow in the feeling man.
Waste not precious time
On the self-inflicted wounds
Of the human race.
What are our problems,
Generated by weakness,
Making life a crushing burden.
The world, a place for pleasure,
Mutated to an old man of the sea
By false imagination.
Our best friend, Time, most cruelly abused
By those it would assist.
Let your watchword be to give and gather joy.
Watch for deceiving snares
That would with endless evil argument
Rob you of a hour's conversation.

Cynic

Sometimes the mind becalmed,
At rest for one brief space
From the crossing winds,
Can contemplate the placid seas
Almost in unbelieving wonder.
For the fragile coracle that carries us
Through the shooting rapids of existence
Seems never to lie at ease,
But, assailed continuously,
By dangers new and old
Tumbles perilously onwards,
Till one of Mirza'a doors flies open,
Sending craft and sailors to their end.
So live life, and when peace comes, be at peace.

Midnight

Now I should switch off the light and sleep,
For the day's work is over. But, instead,
I take up paper and a pen and look
Around the room that is a feeble shade
Of home. The books upon the windowsill
Are old companions, and the place is littered
With fragments taken from the real home
Where I once lived in a pure atmosphere.
Now my task to take the fragments with me,
With the stronger bonds of sacred union,
And plant them like some hardy fertile roots
In the welcoming soil of another land,
So that our lives should not be separate strife,
But shared troubles, and united joy.

As You Like It

To come into the world unwilling,
Struggle to learn self-preservation,
Then, cast out from the mother's warmth
And father's protecting touch
Into a grasping world where pity
Is a fault. To fight yet onwards
Clutching a bauble here, a nettle there,
In a vain attempt at satisfaction.
To take a willing partner at some stage
To share existence and, perhaps bring more,
Themselves unwilling, to while away the time.
To yield one's soul in one concluding breath
And, pray God, realise long before
That moment, here we are to live and love.

CHILDREN

A chld's a pretty picture
    And innocent.
Your baby gives you pleasure
    With her mischievous merriment

A little thing's the finest cure
    For a tiring day.
She has the power with her smile pure
    To bring oblivion as you join her play.

Uncanny the understanding
    Of a mite of two.
See affection growing
    As she looks at you.

Crying when you leave her
    And happy when you return,
Who else has she to love her?
    You are her world, and she is part of you,
And you from her will learn.

FATHER

Sitting there so peacefully asleep,
<u>You</u> have been through the fray and rest
At last, now knowing the way clear to live
Well, in accordance with reality.
Man takes a puny step away from earth
And all at once appears a tiny speck
Against the background of the universe,
And his life a paltry instant in an age
Of time. To ravage, slaughter, terrorize,
For fleeting power, to grasp the thorny sceptre
Only to plunge into the remorseless pit
Of death. Or if a righteous man to prove
His right and perish. You alone have learned
Life is to brief to know how just your case.

Snow

Crisp dull delicate white mantle
Over the green landscape.
A wintry mist blots out the city sounds.
Graceful blanched lace-like veils
Demurely shield the trees
From the harsh eye,
Coating bare branches with feathery gossamer.
Sombre sky foreboding snow,
Sad cry of the seabirds
Driven landward by the thundering ocean.
In vain their fellows of the woods
Specks of black against a wan horizon
Search the hard hostile earth for food
Beneath the grey trunks of hoary-headed pines.
These wintry robes woven delicate
Cloak the world with an eerie stillness.
And frost hides the cruelty of the bitter time.

On Listening to Baroque Music

Stride up and down the scales of melody
Exploring deep recesses of the soul.
The instruments are of another time,
And paint a gentleness that was not then.
One wonders how the fragile mind survived
In those rough times which wrought such soul-pierce works,
The harpsichord much truer than the piano,
The strings attempting to outreach each other
In lyric flow of centuries-old sound,
They touch us many times. The haunting notes
Of Purcell's sad sweet songs and Bach's cantatas
Echo the grandeur of an age to come
When one inspired by Heaven deaf old man
Should transcend frailty with majestic art.

TOIL

Anguish, suffering, tortuous pain
Yield to bright hard sterile steel,
But there are other agonies
When human love is sundered
By the parting life.
Kindly rays and hollows on the brow
Betray a furrowed mind.
Rough labour-worn firm weathered hands
Are sealed with honour,
But other scars mark the struggling past,
Thoughts, deeds, creations, even masterpieces,
Are these the finer parts of man?
No master spirit's book's so precious
As his own life-blood.

THE AGE OF THE ALTOGETHER

The age of pseudo-art has come
When it's unfashionable to rhyme.
It's not the rage to harmonize
On manuscript or canvas. Lies
Hold the ring of reputation
And no man knows his proper station.
The less your 'work' is 'understood,'
The more the critics find it good,
And grammar-less disordered gibberish
Has usurped the language English,
While scrap iron from decaying motors
Makes the fame of rising sculptors,
And varied garbage and assorted waste
Mark the artist's cultivated taste.
Culture is in the altogether
But where's the little boy the wiser
To save the world from knavery.
Poor Andersen, we have surpassed thee!

ON THE CONCEPTION OF ART

Who knows the travails of the untrammelled mind
When seized by an urge of unknown origin
To realize by word, note, stroke of brush
Some soulful beauty until then obscured,
Potential, hidden budding of the brain
Its force released along a neuro-channel
To find expression in a human form.
Pleasure yielding to the senses common
To all spectators, eye and ear at one
In strange unwonted sense of satisfaction,
In hearing what we cannot say in words,
In reading what we think but cannot write,
In seeing, listening to the aesthetic forms
Created by the unearthly part of man.

PROGRESS

Slow, faltering laborious body
Housing a restless mind
Straining at its earthly leash.
The mind no frontiers knows
Except those by the Almighty fixed,
A millionaire, a milliard miles
Are the same in its conception.
If to think were to have done,
But then our own inadequacies
With jarring steel reality
Stifle our flowing thoughts.
Still the grand lure of a great achievement
Looms on the skyline like a jewel of promise
For many who deserve the name of man.

Night and Day

How silence can be peace or war,
A soothing calm or ominous pause.
The mind can think, the body brace itself
Against misfortune, or relax content.
All the grasping, striving race of man
Immobilized beneath a soundless sky,
A natural truce until the raw commotion
Of existence relentlessly resumes.
It is an hour most suited to the lone
Philosopher or dreamer, unquenched flame
Of creativity, when the common world
Lies vacant, and the elements appear
In the unspoiled mantle of creation,
Beckoning you in the brief spell of night.

Society

Not cloistered life for an eternity,
But warm close-bonded unity
Weaves the fabric of existence.
No harsher penance
Than to clutch greedily at glory,
See the false prize glitter in nerveless hand,
As death remorseless drives despairing
Down to a sunless land.
Those in whom the secrets of your mind
Are blended in inexplicable love,
Your thoughts, hopes, sufferings and joys entwined
In theirs, as if the Lord had woven
That precious thread into your skein of life.
You hold the key, so guard it well, and live.

SPACE

Violet impenetrable dark,
Yet pierced by pinpoint light
Flickering surely to earth
Through the velvety night.

Gleaming belt of Orion,
Steady guide of the Plough,
Not the sun's living warmth
But a cold distant glow

Defying distance and time,
Dimension and man
Eternally seeking
The key to the Plan

Of how, why, whence and where
Comes the nebula haze,
Delving into the slumbering ether
For knowledge, or praise.

TO PARNELL

Lone voice in the wilderness of politics
In vain you sacrificed your worthy life
In homeland dreams of national liberation.
Honour beware when you approach the door
That leads into the coucils of the great,
For only plot and counter-plot hold sway
When the volume of the prize destroys morality.
Yet, the principle for which you lived is deathless,
And forms the rallying cry for many a people
Struggling beneath the iron boot of tyranny
To live in freedom, even the ways of God.
'No man has the right to fix the boundary
To the march of a nation.' The oppressor
Shall live to see his captive rise indomitable.

In Admiration of RLS

Who knows whether it's braver for the mind
To take the road that leads to self-fulfillment,
Or to spend life like some poor automaton,
Unquestioning in slavish repetition
Of meaningless tasks, lacking both the knowledge
And will to live. There is no finer man
Than he the master of his own existence,
A social idler but a private dynamo,
To gladden the heart of the apologist.
You had a way of writing that your words
Struck through the fiibres of your reader's thoughts.
You are of a time when the joy of conversation
Was the prime vehicle of philosophy,
And all your essays speak the praise of writing.

Spring Slush

Tell me the way to the spring,
  Is it by the warming air,
By the call of the woodland dove
  Peeping crocus or daffdil fair?
Tell me the way to the spring.

Tell me the way to the spring,
  Is it by the chattering rooks,
By the magpie's plumes so pert,
  For he prides himself on his looks?
Tell me the way to the spring.

Tell me the way to the spring,
  Is it by the lambs in the fold,
By the bright grass or the forester's song,
  Herds pasture-bound or the sun-speckled cold?
Tell me the way to the spring.

Tell me the way to the spring,
  Is it by the flooding hill streams,
Sleepy mole in the daylight or forests awake
  Or our emerging from northern dreams,
Is not that the way to the spring?

LIVING

Still, stirring,
Fresh awakening,
Rising, falling,
Thought steadying,
Cooled longing,
Fanned flaming,
Eternal desiring,
Never reaching,
Always dreaming,
Beaten, swaying,
Clutching, clinging,
Breathless living,
Awareness, breathing,
Dim returning.
Mortal being,
This is your living essence.

Snow

False sky-sent beauty
Falling softly, silently,
Swirling and graceful,
Evanescent and fanciful,
Viewed through the window
From the warmth of the fireglow.
Each branch and grass blade
Are richly inlaid
With carpetted pure
Of cold-jewelled nature.
Fluttering flakes alight
On each twig in sight,
Transformed to pale clusters
Of feathery fingers.
Ominous cloudiness
Threatens the wilderness.
Put your foot through the threshold
To an alien world,
Where footfalls sound noiseless
And frosted breath motionless
In this still air.
Shiny cheeks, glistening hair.
With melting droplets
From tree-icy coronets
Of snow-diamond crystal.
The traffic's snail crawl
On the treacherous road,

For this lovely allowed
No warmth in her smile.
Her chilling embrace
Ice-maiden's your face,
And the warm living earth,
Bringing woe to the hearth.
Her glacial beauty
Does not mask winter's cruelty,
And the pale virgin tapestry
Over meadow and city
Brings more sorrow and suffering
Than poem or painting.

Subsistence

Born struggling, destined to hurtle onwards,
Looking neither right nor left nor upwards,
Transformed into computerised machine,
No reason and no purpose to its being,
And, as he tumbles blindly through his life
No time but for a narrow, headlong strife.
All is a shadow round him,
The world a formless phantom,
A setting sun, a cloudless sky,
Rare autmun tints and mountain majesty,
Remain an untapped mystery,
Deaf alike to hope and suffering,
To cry of trampled heart or call to loving.
Ignominy, oblivion, await a milliard such
Whom the secrets of existence never touch.

A Sonnet

The sceptered forest rising by the lake,
The regal diadems of nature's crown
Await the splendour of her coronation
Acclaimed by fluted note from feathered neck

Of songsters from the south, and dove and hawk,
Plumage shimmering, and bright-eyed in unison,
Their mistress nature calls them to her own,
Spring festival of joy to re-awake

The splendour of the past in rose of night,
Fresh promise springing from the thawing earth,
Life-giving scented showers of April sky

Fall soothing cool through velvet roseate light,
As sun falls westward in her fading warmth
Upon young life's hot brow with gentle sigh.

Time

Pale phantom moon through fleeting clouds
Scudding through the heaven sea,
Glowing crescent, luminous shrouds,
Silent now the world, alone with me.

The cold revealing light of history,
Our nearest universal neigbour globe,
A world unknown to life, a fantasy
Beyond our reach until today. A probe

Of feeble earthlings, amd the dusty pits
And ash-grey lunar surface scarred by time,
Echoing long-dead fires whose violence fits
The mood of man, bred in a violent clime,

Stand gaunt, revealed in cold reflected form,
A sign to science, but no poetry,
Still guide to sailors in a darkening storm,
And now unveiled, a greater mystery!

YOUTH

Must there be a break
Between the old life and the new,
Or should there be a link?
There is. This ocean dark dull blue

That bears me east and south
To promise, yet unknown,
Proving to me that both
Form one life for me, my own

Whose hours may pass in loathsome idleness,
To see the rising and the setting sun
Without one deed or thought to that great purpose
For which we live. To think no victory won

In lifelong struggle. And let no day pass
But you can say you fought it valiantly
As befits one whom the Lord did bless
With one brief time to treasure jealously.

THE TRAVELLER

From my carriage window seen
Scars left by endless rails,
Nature's tangled tortuous green
Adorns the parapets with trails

Of bramble, tumbleweed. Then swaying
Sudden into coal-stained black,
As if it were animate and saying
Keep time along my timeless track.

No wonder at the rushing hills
Or solitary kestrel on his perch,
The power pulling onward wills
My destination neaer. Scorch

Of smoke at every tunnel port
Betrays the futile, frantic haste,
To see the sights by rail - time short,
Might just as well cross desert waste.

DAWN

It is then true that on this godless earth
There is a power that through the ether moves
Unseen, but not unfelt by those who seek
Its aid in their weak course, afraid less sins
Of the children be visited on their sires,
Petty evil returned for good, and mindless deeds
Mar the rare purity of a happy home.
There is a purpose to this scheme of things,
And that is why you live and breathe and eat
And talk and sleep and move your mortal form.
His will shall be done, amd it were best
For the sake of those you hold most dear,
And even for yourself, your peace and joy,
To bend your errant soul in love and shame,
Craving His pardon, and His blessing too
To steady the wanderer and uplift the good.

FRAILTY

I have not felt more urgent in my task
Since body frailty hemmed me on all sides.
The given span depends on many links,
Break one, break the sequence, and the life.
Yet no deformity can hold the mind
From living, and the willing soul from joy.
Beauty and knowledge flourish radiantly
Where barren stony ground defies survival
By feebler plants. To will over infirmity
Nor face each trial with rebel discontent,
Though not to fear or suffer is not human,
To value more what you may be denied,
One only of the many gifts of God,
To rule yourself, if you would conquer worlds.

Forest Night

Fragrant carpet underfoot
In the dark pinewood,
Lightning flash and thunder loud
Pierce the moonless, racing cloud.
How alive the forest,
With scurrying in nest
On trunks of oak.
Small furry folk -
Reynard stealthy slinks,
And old Brock shuffles,
Their storm-lit eyes
Gleaming in the starless night,
Searching some farmyard prize
In the spectre moonlight.
Dark bulky forms the clouds
Voyage above the trees,
Evanescent shrouds
Over the earth, while he breeze
Of autumn soothing soft
Ruffles the swaying firs.
Grey squirrel chattering aloft,
The unseen nightingale airs
Its gladdening voice.

The nightjar's discord
Mingles with the lesser noise
Of the woodland family,
Slowly stilling nature's notes
In each high nest and earthy burrow
Bringing rest until the marrow.

On looking at a painting
by Seán Ceitinn

Cold blue grey white green,
Hot red orange yellow,
Clashing shimmering sheen
Of the sprite ocean billow.

Chill twilight purple
On warm tawny sunset,
Wind and waves merging ripple
In the calm evening quiet.

Only one lonely steamer
Marks the scene for man,
Black against millionfold colour
Of the Mediterranean sun

And the sea. One wispy grey trail
Wends its way from the ship to the sky
In the strokes of that brush so frank yet so frail
Lies the genius of artistry.

Evening at Versailles

Bent low beneath a moonlit love,
Sharp shaft to pierce the heart,
As each soul with the other strove
To join each separate part,

Laughing god on pearly pedestal
Bathed in a soft night glow,
Cheerful cherub gambling all
On the innocents below,

Silvery fairy fountain drops
Raised in a gracious arc,
Fireflies mingling, sparkling steps
In the luminous dark.

No earthly paradise to show
Such visionary wonder
As two souls joined in joy, but how
To find oneself such splendour?

FATHERHOOD

Play, little child,
  Laugh, little girl,
With your dancing smile
  And each soft brown curl
Over trusting eyes,
  Gleefully shouting
    As you scatter your toys
All over the drawing room floor.
Hide and seek by the door,
Run to your Daddy when he comes home,
  Fetching his slippers
    Then scrambling and climbing
      On to his knee
Telling archly in whispers
  Of the birdie you saw,
And the games that you played
  How you held doggie's paw,
How you like marmalade,
Till thoughts of the City fade from your mind,
Happier with her than a king of mankind.

Companionship

The finest moments that we know
Are those shared with another, though unreasonable
It seems to need some second individual
To draw the utmost pleasure from the galaxy
Of gentle pastimes that adorn the world.
But on no happier ear did merry notes
Of gay Gioacchino fall than that of lover
Mounting the silken stair to mistress' heart,
Nor did Amadeus gentle thread more warmly
Than to the hearth of a contented home.
Which two who know the joys of company
Gaze not with pity on the lone composer,
Or the solitary admirer of the daffodils.

COUNTRYSIDE

Azure glitter on the thatch
  Sheltering the marten's nest,
Familiar creak of rusty larch
  As you venture forth in quest.

A day of expectation
  When the honeyed air hums calm
For youthful inspiration
  Beneath sun-golden arm.

Walk through the bowing corn
  With your face freshened by the breeze,
No sound save shepherd horn,
  No sight but can please,

Whether of hill, lake or fold,
  Wild lapwing, or skylark above,
Rush forward and greet her to yield
  To the welcoming warmth of your love.

ENNISKERRY

A day in the country by the cascade stream
With only rocks and woods to meet the eye,
Green ferns overlapping at the water edge,
With rushes sheltering the waterfowl.
The hunter's cry over the forest giants,
The cold shock as you hit the torrent water,
And watch the smooth speckled trout glide swiftly
Downstream with leaves and branches on the current.
Wild bluebell nods its sturdy fragrant head
Beside river bank, and saffron primrose greets
The morning sun, and all the spring flora send
Their messages of wakening with incense
Of the budding pines. Now there's a sanctuary
For the solitary soul from the soul-starved city.

There's None so Blind

A pleasant evening conversation
Is a pastime for thoughtful mind,
To share experience of another,
Pages of a book to read mankind.
Far finer than the printed page
Is the art of understanding,
And wiser than the cloistered sage
Is he who reads not boks but hearts.
The herd rush on past beauties unrevealed,
Blessed the few for whom the world's unveiled.

Meaningful

All of us fear for our life and our limb,
   And sometimes one goes missing,
But please let it never get so grim
   That we lose the parts for kissing.

Strange man to amble through centre boutique
   And not with bored dull glazed stare,
But thinking so personal for your chic
   When choosing what you might wear.

It can make a man proud to feel your arm
   Hold tight, sometimes both, to my own,
Easier as one to repel all harm
   When together through years we have grown.

Getting and spending, Wordsworth said,
   We lay waste our powers,
Useless baubles, honours, instead
   Of savouring together-hours.

We have long left that iron-road station
   Where started unwinding rail's life,
The tickets are single, the destination
   Inevitable, complexed by strife.

Why do we chase ephemeral ghosts
    When so much fun's to be had?
Never be bored when there are those hosts
    Of things that make glad.

D'Artagnan's marshal baton fell
    Futile from nerveless hand,
Better could he of quietude tell
    With soulmate-friends. hand in hand.

Too late, too late, and let not the bell toll
    When you realize what it's about,
For then it's far past when they call the roll,
    For your soul will have left, with a shout.

We've only one chance, if a second, but rare
    To love and to hold and see light,
Joys to unite and troubles to share
    Make us happy and strong day and night.

FLIRT

Lure on frail beauty of a moment's glance
And lead nan's heart a merry dance.
Your time is far too brief.
You must gamble all, leave all to chance.

Yet your power is a transient shade,
And your loveliness will fade
From scented flower to dull green leaf,
And so you are afraid.

Knowing yourself both strong and weak
Makes you forever seek
A husband-honest kiss,
While daily conquests make your week.

For that is the object of your life
And to that end is all your strife
Hoping for the homely bliss
That comes with being a wife.

The Electronic Age

I get a terrible shock
When something actually works,
It was only eleven o'clock
Where the rail information line lurks.

The voice mail's disemobodied selections
Brought my sigh and the usual groan,
But a <u>human</u> gave instant directions,
Never made such a score on the phone!

So my railcard has entered the ether,
And, if Royal Mail works on that day,
Come sunny or turbulent weather
On iron road I'll be wending my way!

Alastair Cooke

They coouldn't let him be the first to read
The final letter from across the pond,
That calm and cool and unique voice of reason,
Week 'Letter from America' beyond.

Terrible reflection of our age,
To contemplate the aftermath of life,
Ghouls wouldn't let the poor man rest in peace,
But threw his bones to winds of timeless strife.

The moron age where nothing is of value;
Even those from death camps of the east
Cower from predations of the throwbacks
Who prove the origin of man is beast.

Concentration-camp or soldier who survived
The horrors of the struggle to be free
Can look forward to being murdered, mugged or raped
In this mockery of human liberty.

Indifference is no substitute for tolerance,
Democracy does not mean lose control.
Where are we, when the criminals, not the victims,
Are those for whom the bleeding-heart bells toll.

US

A woman shouldn't have to work
You say, and you are right,
From seven a.m.(you don't shirk)
Till twelve o'clock at night.

For me, a man, it's just the same,
But I will stop 'fore one,
For we both know life's not a game
But truly can be fun!

I now beneath the duvet creep
Like you, for nowt is worse
Than shortening our hours of sleep
By writing silly verse!

FATHER

It's four months since I lost you in this world,
And only hope to find you in the next.
I pray you both are re-entwined in love,
With Almighty love for you, who kept His ways.

You are the source of everything I am,
That is, those parts of me that pass for good.
The advice I did not take I paid so dear.
I cannot interrupt you any more.

I am so sad I never had your patience,
Your strength, your good, your courage, your nobility.
You left your brutal school at seventeen,
Yet were the deepest man I ever knew.

Your quiet, wise words ever in my ear,
Even though I could be quite distrait.
Your goodness shone in everything you did,
And all your life was open to the sky.

You are the only one who had no need
To hide or feel ashamed for any deed,
You truly said your life's an open book,
But others' books are full of leaves uncut.

You were the epitome of love,
Of selfless duty and self-sacrifice,
As son, as brother, husband and, thank God,
It was our chance you were our Father, too.

Your grace and wit and charm were never-ending,
Always the lifeblood of the souls you met.
You had an insight into human minds,
Untouched by modern dull philosophers.

Even when you were about to leave,
I came to our home, so sad to find on floor
Library cards, books you had meant to read,
Most the biographic and historic.

How could a man of such deep understanding,
Such culture, education, all self-taught,
Still humbly seek for further information,
Modesty matching solely search for truth?

Your kindness endless, your forgiveness sublime,
You were so tolerant of others' frailties.
Your friends were truly by adoption tried.
Loyalty you inspired in all who knew you right.

I know the path of life is full of suffering,
No-one can escape its harsh embraces,
Yet, somehow, you smiled through harrowing life-pain,
Somehow you stayed indomitable within.

Much easier for the thick-skinned of those days,
But you were sensitive and easily hurt.
Yet when misfortune cast you to the ground,
You rose, alone, with none to soothe your sorrow.

You, who had no scientific training,
Forty years this year you gave advice,
It was the source of my entire career,
And now at forefront of the world's research.

Highbrow or low, all you met you charmed,
All good men cared for you, the bad respected,
You to your people always remained true,
From monkish school until you left this life.

It grieves me to my soul I could not be
As gentle, tolerant, patient, as you breathed,
Yet loved you heart and soul with all my might,
Because of the goodness of your living essence.

God tells us we must honour father, mother,
He does not tell us or command our love,
But, would all have a Father such as you,
Then they would understand the pain that fills my soul.

Enjoy!

You think you've no time,
But, please, read my small rhyme:
To stay in a hole
Is bad or the soul,
And, though you were late,
And things complicate,
Yet it's good to be there
For the people who care,
For, believe me, they do
Care the same way for you.
So, let's be together,
Come fair or foul weather.
It's not true that we pay
For going away,
Wherever we go
There's something to do,
So don't let us boast of it,
But just make the most of it.
Our greatest need?
More haste, less speed.
Don't overdo it
If you want to get through it,
And, if you know poker,
Play your ace, not a joker.
The chancers avoid work,
The doers, they never shirk,
And, if you're the boss,

Then don't give a toss,
Let others give cover,
So you can recover.
Here's to life, and its pleasure,
And, for us, far more leisure!

DAD

They say winter will be severe
With northern bone-chill cold,
But no-one warned the buds of spring
Whose shoots so straight unfold.

The sad year past saw planting late.
He would have wished it so.
'Dum spiro spero' was his word
Who never ceased to grow.

No-one with a soul can thrive
Flowerless through the year,
And best, he said, are those we raise
Ourselves to give us cheer.

Even near his latest hour
He took my arm, though slow,
To savour garden fruitfulness,
To see life's growing glow.

Everything he knew he taught,
To us he has bequeathed
The deepest insights of great thought
In gentle words he wreathed.

A truly noble gentle man
Did all he met inspire.
His mighty vision, when I can
My sorrow bear, make clear.

It's still too much to think about
The goodness that he was,
And so for now my tears I'll keep
For roses in a vase.

'I do not mind what you may plant
So long as they are roses.'
Since I was small I do recall
March pruning of those roses.

All were scented, delicate,
No greenfly, perfect form,
Dublin to London did translate
The skills of garden home.

It was his pleasure till near time
To walk his garden round,
To sit in summer, watch the bees
Buzzing the lavender ground.

My heart's so full I cannot pen
More words of Dad this time.
I only hope he sees the buds
I've planted for springtime.